Metaphors of the Mind © 2024 Bini John

All rights reserved.

No part of this publication may be reproduced, stored in a retrieval system, or transmitted, in any form or by any means, electronic, mechanical, photocopying, recording or otherwise, without the prior written permission of the presenters.

Bini John asserts the moral right to be identified as the author of this work.

Presentation by *BookLeaf Publishing*

Web: www.bookleafpub.com

E-mail: info@bookleafpub.com

ISBN: 9789360944711

First edition 2024

AF797656

Metaphors of the Mind

Bini John

BookLeaf Publishing
India | USA | UK

To my family, for your trust in me, I dedicate this collection.

ACKNOWLEDGEMENT

To "The force that through the green fuse drives the flower", and my family.

PREFACE

The poet holds a lens to her life and transfers into words what is most challenging as she proceeds. In the process, the poet realizes that words not only just act like the vessels of her experience, but also force her to inspect her own life and its details. To the poet, these details are intentionally forgotten for they hurt and words do not spare them either. Words thus play a dual role in the poet's life.

I am No poet

I am no poet, yet I want to write
Words do charm me to my desk
Yet I do stare at the empty paper
Blank and scary, as I sit.

The rhyme and the reason
The fame and the name
All drove me to my desk
Yet, I am no poet to write a word.

An epic I do want
Void it is that I create
Great tales are all already told
Closed in my room, nothing did I find.

Let words play, I do wish
But my desk still stays bare
I am no poet, yet I want to write
Tales and thoughts gleaned from life.

My Pen

My pen is like a plow
It tills and toils the earth I live.
Crushes the clods of thoughts
And uproots the weed that's rooted.

Like a scalpel, it cuts open
The veins of sorrowful tales.
Keen and sharp, it swishes through
The deepest wounds I still hide.

Like a sieve, it sifts me through
Splits me up in coarser lumps
What it leaves is all the pain
Of the tears that I never shed.

Yet I do want to write
Exhume and mourn again
Pick those scabs and heal again
For my pen writes me forth.

Desperate Attempts

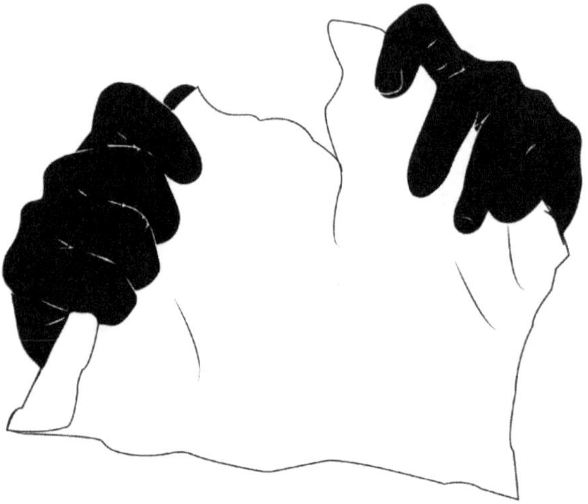

As I sat there in the deepest thoughts of mine
I saw a shadow hiding yet so dark
The dance of thoughts it hide under
If only I could push it yonder.

I long to pen those thoughts of mine
They need to guide me in the murk
I battle the shadows they hide under
To shine some light on my wonder.

There I sat upon the promises of the wine
The juices of the disconsolate musings
Yet they refuse to come and glide
Oh, the shadow reminds her to hide.

Her battles are in vain
Her pen writhes in her hand
Her papyrus weighs under her longing
If only I could fuel that quill
If only I could write in thrill!

Just Like You, I made some New Year's Resolutions

Just like you, I had New Year's resolutions.
Just like that, I thought I could follow it!
Just like that, I forgot I am a married woman!
Just like that, I ignored I am a mother!

I fell into the sink whole of dishes,
the ever-piling piles of dishes,
the never-ending chore of washing.

The foam on the sponge cleaned all the dishes,
The foam on the sponge cleaved my heart.
Just like that, I forgot my resolutions!

The pound of the disposer crushed all the bones
The sound of the disposer brushed aside my
hopes.
Just like that, I remained the lame old me!

The flow of the tap water cleansed all the dishes.
The flow of the persistent tap water washed
away the new me.
Just like that, I drowned in the chores!

Just like that, I thought I could do poems!
Just like that, I thought words would flow!
Just like that, I couldn't be a writer!

Women Now

I am my Aladdin.
Knowing the magic words;
Knowing the power.
Knowing the genie.
It is hard to be squished into silence,
Knowing the magic words.

It is my silence
Burning the lamp.
The prettier it looks,

The brighter I burn.
Spilt out, I can,
I can do everything.
Squished into silence
I can light the lamp.
I am my Aladdin
With my magic words of freedom,
Silenced within me.

I am burning at both ends
It is still the Promethean legacy.
It is a choice,
But when did I?

It Takes Courage to Let the Ship Sink

You know, it's actually no ship
The low branches wrap her around
She broods over the tidal bore
Halted and faded, she's been there for a while.

There's a story how it got there!
Happily paddled by them young
She thrust forth bubbling in joy
And the winds Swayed her in joy.

The hands found their rhythm,
Without fathoming the spasm.
Water gushed up from the chasm
The boat moved with the system.

One looked at the other
And took his hands farther
The other did muster
All the strength moving further.

The boat found a course
Far and new, yet it continued.
One chose to continue
The other did discontinue.
Oh the wind is pushing
The water is gushing
The rowing is now biting.

The low branches swooped down to kiss
As though in an effort to comfort
Yet it was an effort to stay afloat!

The unset sun saw her still
That she now let it go by will
It's now hidden and still
It's a tiny sailing boat.

Some Thoughts to Toy

If to remain in a state of joy
There are means to employ
Seek not to destroy
A moment to enjoy.

If to remain and enjoy
Please don't annoy
Keep up the convoy
Stop not to be coy.

If to remain and enjoy
Please don't deploy
Seek sure to destroy
A heart that is a decoy.

Broken Self

I glued together my broken self
My tears it shed but sure it hardened
Later I added a lesson to patch.

Fragile I started, facing the world
The choices I made, did end mistake
Often I found me in my shadow,
Broken and scattered on the floor.

I picked up the pieces and added a thought
A faint lesson to stick them together
A little wiser every day I got.

Eyes sparkled with dreams
Often I stood, in the coldest spot
Arid and dreary, most of them turned
A heart-wounded, stubbornly bickers.

Burnt to ashes, yet did rise the phoenix
From the ashes of pain, new wings devise.
A person once broken, stronger, and scarred.

Acceptance

There are several magic words:
Please and thank you one could say
Acceptance, I will say.

Accept it as it is
Is the biggest fight you fight.
At least try it, I will too.

I wish I could do it all at once
Be the one for him in life
Accept did I, I could not.

I wish I could be it all
Accept did I, though with pain
That I am just one in all.

I wish I could be
The preference of the one

Later did I see, I cannot.

The dearest did I yearn
To accept that I will not
At least try it, I should do.

That I am just one another
Is the hardest I could learn
Accept it as it is, is the biggest fight I still do.

Choices

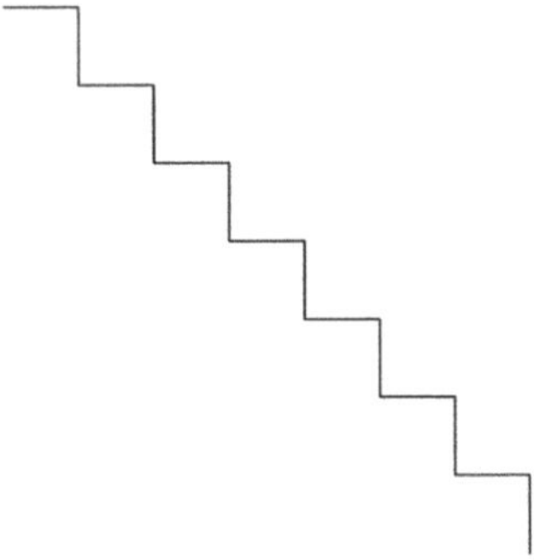

Choices to be made, always in life.
This or that, that's the question.
Good or bad, never taunt our minds
Easy or difficult is all that matters to us.

Choices once made, ways once left
Persons once forgotten, paths never taken
Are the thorns that our mind is stuck at.
Now or never is all that matters though.

Meaning

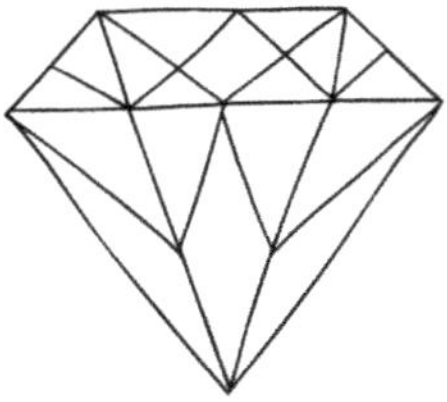

The moment I go silent
I see a thousand new meanings
The floating, shapeless meanings.

Questions asked twice, can they be answered?

Meaning, I keep searching
Shapeless it is, yet sure in existence.
What is meaning?
Is that truth?

Words

I have closed my mouth, but words
Refused to stay within.
Out they went, twisting my hands,
Through my sighs and twitching muscles.
They groped in the thickening air
For they were spirits denied of bodies.
They failed to communicate
And sure they did desiccate.

The moist feeling of love
The brightest shine of life
The curve of a sorrow
The charm of a morning
They lost it all, my poor words.

I have started a search, but words
Where do they hide?

The Migraine Brain

In those days of shine, down I went under the pillow
But the click of the mouse and the tick of the watch
Pound me further, through the fluffness of the pillow.

My eyes are shut, but my eyes are burning bright
Their fire is scorching me from their depths.
I need not a torch, for I am blinded by the flash.

Whispers echo like a roaring tide
Oft I plead to a shadow to abide
Reality shimmers as auras dance.

The kaleidoscope of emotions bears me down
In the migraine's grip relentless and grand
In the shadowed realm, the sufferer succumbed.

Yet, from the shadows resilience rise
As the storm yields, bit by bit
The warrior rises and shines.

The Moment

You ever had that feeling?
You are not hurt by all the insults hurled at you
Or the landslide of emotions that you are thrown under
But that trickling feeling that it hurt no more?

Well, that's where I met me, the new me
That's where I grew less bitter
And that's where I wish to be.

The dewy thought sat there still
Glistening in that ray of hope
Better did I feel, as it stayed
Often the blaze stole it away.

The path is to a temperate world
Where logic mildly leads the way
Do I dare to, is a quest
Most I care is moving beside.

The Fatigue of Words

Young Bilingual:

I speak two tongues
One knows the other
One leans on the other.

They take turns formally
They fall out of tune casually
One must stay in its lane
One must play in vain.

I am a bilingual
One that loves both her tongues
Clasped each other in one hold
They grew up together.

Their play, she nurtured
Their delay she suffered
Their growth she preferred.

One evokes the other
One provokes the other
One is me, the other is me too.

Migrant bilingual:

I have half a tongue
Words no more march in line
One has to step aside
For one has to sustain.

One lost its charm
One lost its warmth
One fallen apart
One needs to be sullen!

The migrant resolution:

I got boxes for my tongues
With clearly defined borders
Where one can and one cannot
They know well their lane!

The tongue longs the tango
Yet stays still in limbo.
One yearns the lingo
Both long the tango.

I speak two languages
I speak one or the other.

The Essay of a Day

Bini John
On Contract

I wake up
I rush
I wake up little ones
I convince one to wake up
I convince one to go to school
I rush
I pee
I rinse

I make breakfast
I persuade one to eat
I persuade another to finish eating
I see them off
I brush
I comb
I make tea
I make breakfast
I make for the other
I drink tea
I eat
Oh, well, I sat.
I read
I do homework
I grade papers
I walk
I stretch
I rush
I shower
I dress up
I teach
I train writing
One couldn't log in
I teach tech
One couldn't understand
I help comprehend
I explain
I use strategies
I assign work

I review writing
Oh, well, I sat.
I rush
I drive
I tutor
I support tutors
I read
I write
I create an environment
I rush
I drive
I am home, am I?
I cook
I clean
I make tea
I eat lunch
I gulp down tea
I rush
I teach
I teach language
I teach
I train writers
One couldn't log in
I teach tech
One couldn't understand
I help comprehend
I explain
I use strategies
I assign work

I review writing
I am done.
I clean
I listen to one
I argue with another
I encourage both
I need to be there.
I rush
I shower
I go to bed
I plan
I read
I do homework
I sleep.
I wake up
I am on contract.

The Essay of a Day
Part II: The Professorial Feedback
Your thesis isn't clear
[Well, do I have to?]
You aren't concise.
[Can I?]
Your format is chaotic.
[I write me]
You need to add more information for clarity.
[I missed them in life too]
Your sequencing of events needs tidying up.
[I am on contract]

Dichotomous Life

I woke up, held a glass of water to my mouth, realized I did not wake my girl, so rushed up and gave her a nudge,
came back and cut some veggies then made some tea, I saw my glass of water, brought it close to my lips, and glanced at the rising rays from the east, but I got to rush, rush to the shower to get me ready for the world that is not like me.

The water is too cold, so I set it to that warmth that I miss in that world
Off to which I should go, to make my living so that I could survive.
I get in the shower, and water caresses me with warmth, but I do remember
to wash off all the flavors of my land, of my skin but it is still some brown.

I get out and wrap in alien drapes, home I should find in these, yet here I am.
I turn that stereo on, turn off the rhythm of tales from my heart.
I set my mind on goals for life and off I go to the segmented truth of the day.
I hold my breath and get through it, talk to people like I am there
Part of me rumbling in to be, part of me savvy to not be.
The dichotomous life is real, thus I hold my breath and barely survive.

www.ingramcontent.com/pod-product-compliance
Lightning Source LLC
LaVergne TN
LVHW020003181026
850499LV00041B/1734
9789360944711